THIS VISION JOURNAL BELONGS TO:

FOR THE YEAR:

Ordering Information:
Annabelledura.com

IBSN
979-8-9921608-1-9

WELCOME TO
THE VISION JOURNAL

Welcome to *The Vision Journal*. This process aims to align your actions with what genuinely inspires you, so each new year goal becomes a step toward a life that feels deeply authentic and fulfilling.

In these pages, you'll explore a new approach to goal-setting and vision casting—one that centers on who you're becoming rather than external pressures or expectations.

This process isn't about pleasing others, striving to meet conventional definitions of success, or living up to societal expectations. Instead, it's all about you: tuning into your unique vision, embracing your authenticity, and honoring the values that make you feel alive.

This is a chance to ask yourself questions like, "Where do these goals come from? How do they serve my purpose?"

As you move through this process, you'll notice that your vision isn't just a distant dream; it's an evolving path shaped by your choices, growth, and the clarity that comes from the consistent practice of getting to know yourself and being in communication with what your unique and beautiful life is asking of you.

You'll find there is no "right" or "wrong" way to approach these exercises—only what feels aligned for you. **The Vision Journal process is more than just a checklist of goals; it's a holistic, heart-centered approach to envisioning the future and connecting to yourself.**

The Vision Journal is divided into three parts, each with a unique focus:

Past Year Reflection
Honor the growth and lessons of the past year.

Clarity
Gain insight into your values and what truly matters.

The New Year
Set your vision for the months ahead.

Take your time with each part; this journey is yours to shape. Whether you move through a section a day or dive in all at once, there is no right or wrong way to complete this journal. Move through the prompts at your own pace.

With this, your journey begins. May it be one of growth, clarity, and alignment with your truest self. Here's to a year that lights you up from within.

> It is said that we are each born with a unique vision, a destiny toward which we are aimed. It is also said that we forget this vision the moment we are born... thus we are sent on an elusive lifelong journey of rediscovery. Such is the elusive nature of the vision. It slips away, yet it guides. It appears in strange dreams and surreal images, seemingly unattainable and preposterous. When we are connected to The Vision, we carry an inspired, enchanted aliveness that others recognize. We trust the world and its synchronicities. We walk through new doors into wonderous opportunities. We all want to be near those with vision. They emit energy more potent than any elixir. When we lose connection to the vision, life becomes dull and exhausting, lacking meaning. Bring back the mystery, bring back the dreams.

> - Kim Krans

TABLE OF CONTENTS

SECTION 1: REFLECTION   06

- EVENTS + MEMORIES
- IDENTITY REFLECTION
- WHEEL OF LIFE REFLECTION

SECTION 2: CLARITY   24

- FIND YOUR VALUES
- VALUE REFLECTION
- ENERGY AUDIT

SECTION 3: NEW YEAR   50

- JOURNAL PROMPTS
- BRAIN DUMP
- CELEBRATING YOU
- INTENTION SETTING
- GOAL-SETTING

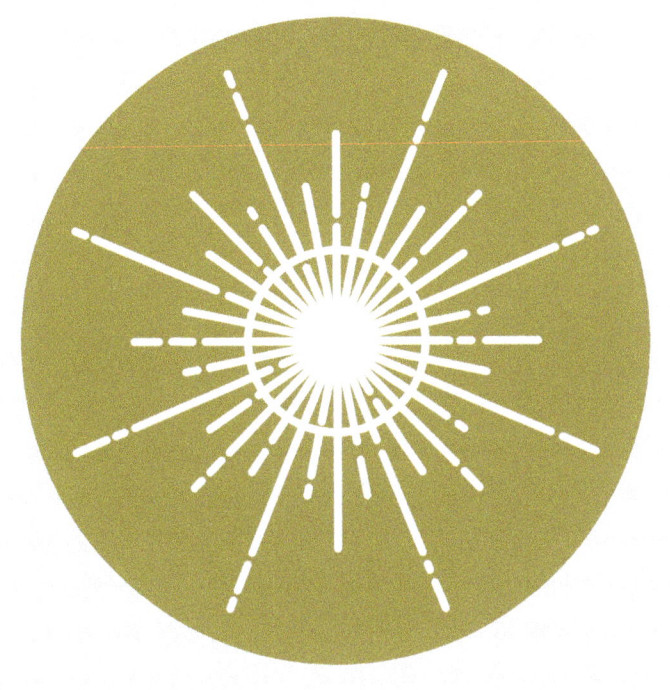

SECTION 1
REFLECTION

EVENTS + MEMORIES

Take the time to reflect on all that you have experienced this year. List both joyful and challenging memories as they have all shaped you to become the person you are today. You can flip through old journals, look through photos on your phone, or revisit your Instagram archive to help jog your memory.

january	february	march

april	may	june

july

august

september

october

november

december

8

REFLECTING ON PAST
EXPERIENCES

Without assigning labels such as good or bad, what are some patterns or themes you noticed after reviewing your year?

What are the 1-3 biggest lessons you learned in this past year?

REFLECTING ON PAST
EXPERIENCES

What will you be leaving behind? If you could speak to the things you are leaving behind, what would you want them to know?

IDENTITY REFLECTION
JOURNAL PROMPTS

WHAT CHALLENGES DID I FACE THIS YEAR?
WHAT DO I NOTICE ABOUT THE PERSON I
BECAME TO OVERCOME THEM?

IDENTITY REFLECTION
JOURNAL PROMPTS

IF I COULD SEE MY LIFE THIS YEAR FROM AN OUTSIDER'S PERSPECTIVE, WHAT WOULD I ADMIRE MOST ABOUT MYSELF?

IDENTITY REFLECTION
JOURNAL PROMPTS

WHAT PART OF MYSELF HAVE I BEEN DENYING OR SUPPRESSING THIS YEAR, AND WHAT WOULD IT MEAN TO FINALLY HONOR THAT PART OF ME?

IDENTITY REFLECTION
JOURNAL PROMPTS

WHAT WOULD I DO DIFFERENTLY IF I KNEW
THAT MY DECISIONS WOULDN'T JUST
TRANSFORM MY LIFE, BUT ALSO THE FUTURE
GENERATIONS OF MY FAMILY OR COMMUNITY?

360° REFLECTION
YOUR LIFE IN BALANCE

Now that you've bravely taken the time to reflect on the events and memories from the past year, it's time to shift gears into a present-moment 360-degree reflection. This exercise will help you to evaluate eight different areas of your life based on how you feel about them today.

In this exercise, you'll take a snapshot of the following areas of life: Spirituality, Career, Mental Health, Physical Health, Relationships, Money, Environment, and Self.

To help you rank each area, ask yourself the following five questions:

- Am I satisfied with this area of my life?
- Do I feel loved, supported, and excited about this area?
- Am I able to fully live out my values in this area?
- Does the way I live in this part of my life feel authentic and true to me?
- Do I need to learn more about this area?

These questions help you rate your satisfaction through love, support, and how much you feel you're expressing your authentic self in each area.

For example, if you're feeling underappreciated at work and unclear about your next steps, you might give Career a lower score. But if you feel free to express yourself, valued, and excited about your career, you'd give it a higher score.

As you reflect, you might have thoughts or ideas about what you'd like to improve or goals you might want to set in the future. There's space on the next page for you to jot down those notes as you move through the exercise. Making a note of how you'd like to help improve the rankings in each area of life will be beneficial to refer to in the goal-setting section later on.

This reflection usually takes about 15-25 minutes, so give yourself the time to really think it through and be honest with yourself.

16

AREAS OF LIFE

Reference this page when completing the following exercise. **You can use the definitions provided or cross them out and write new ones that feel more aligned to you.**

SPIRITUALITY:
Religious or faith-based practices or study.

CAREER:
Your current work or dream job.

MENTAL HEALTH:
The well-being of your emotional and mental state.

PHYSICAL HEALTH:
The well-being of your physical body.

RELATIONSHIPS:
Connections with friends, family, strangers, and lovers.

MONEY:
Your relationship to money; earning, spending, & saving.

ENVIRONMENT:
Physical space around you. your home, office space, etc.

SELF:
Relationship to self. self-actualization, self-love, self-expression, and personal development.

WHEEL OF LIFE

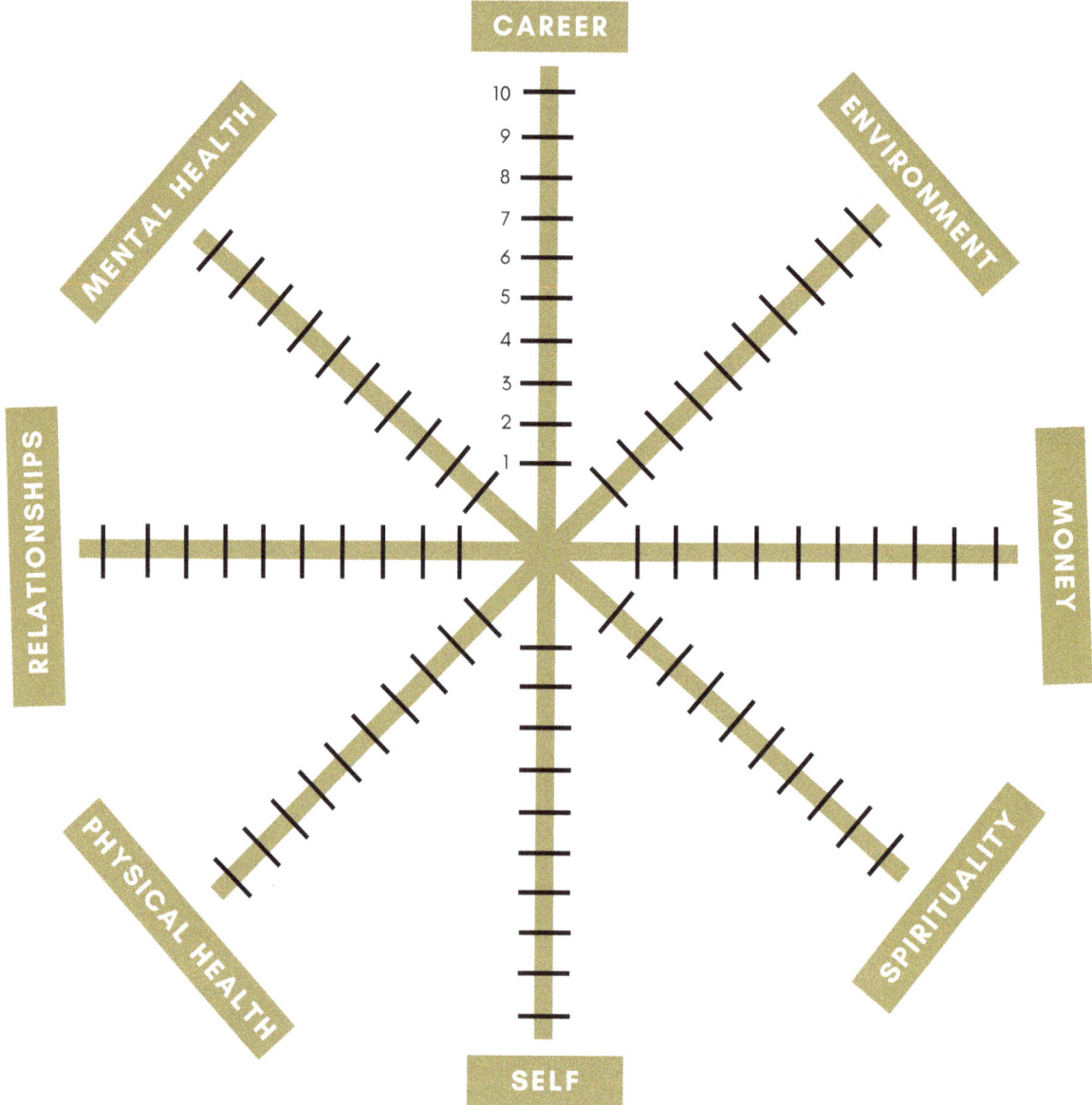

Rate each area of your life 1-10, with 10 being your ideal. Use these questions to reflect on each area of life before rating.

1. Am I satisfied with this area of my life?
2. Do I feel loved, supported, & excited about this area of my life?
3. Am I able to fully live out my values in this area of my life?
4. Does the way I live this area of my life feel fully authentic & true to me?
5. Do I need to learn more about this area of life?

NOTES

CAREER

ENVIRONMENT

MONEY

SPIRITUALITY

SELF

PHYSICAL HEALTH

RELATIONSHIPS

MENTAL HEALTH

REFLECTING ON THE
WHEEL OF LIFE

Were you surprised by any of the results? Why or why not?

21

Identify areas of your life that are ranked highly. What is going well here?

Identify the areas of your life that are ranked low. What is one thing you can do to improve this area of life?

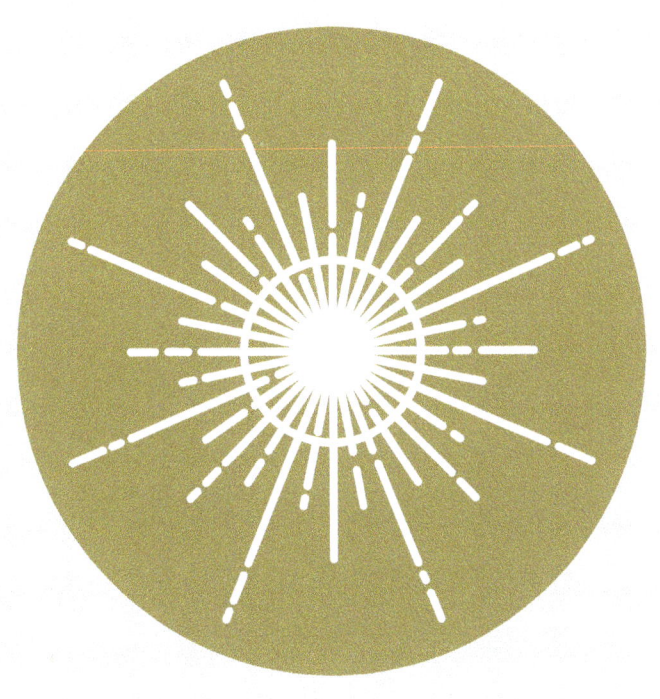

SECTION 2
CLARITY

FIND YOUR VALUES
YOUR NORTH STAR

Every decision you make is motivated by something—either your **values** or your fear. When you are out of alignment it can be harder to discern what is authentic to you, making it easier to follow the persuasive voice of fear.

Misalignment just means being out of integrity with your values. The good news is that getting back into alignment is simple; just begin making decisions that uphold things that are important to you. By doing this exercise, you'll bring the subconscious drivers of your life into your conscious awareness, which allows you to make empowered authentic decisions.

Until you make the unconscious
conscious, it will direct your life
and you will call it fate.

- Carl Jung

THE EXERCISE

In the next few pages, you'll find a list of over 100 character traits and values, with space to add your own. The goal is to narrow this list down to your top three to five values—the core drivers behind most of your decision-making.

Here are some helpful tips to guide you:

1. **Redefine as needed.** If a definition doesn't fully reflect what the word means to you, rewrite it so it resonates with your understanding.
2. **Find common themes.** If you notice several similar words (like *family*, *friendship*, and *community*), try to identify one word that captures the essence of all three. For example, *community* might be the word that best reflects all your relationships.
3. **Set a timer.** If you're feeling overwhelmed or if it's taking too long, set a five-minute timer for each round. This helps you rely on your instincts rather than overthinking.
4. **Feel it out.** As you go through each word, focus on how it feels in your body rather than just what it means intellectually. Words that evoke a strong feeling are likely to be your core values.

It's helpful to do this exercise every six months to track your growth. Your values may naturally shift as life unfolds, reflecting what you're learning and integrating. After completing the values exercise, you'll have the opportunity to dive deeper into each value—exploring what it means to you, how it shows up in your life, and how it can guide your future decisions.

INSTRUCTIONS

Round 1: To start, read through the entire list of values and circle the ones that feel the most important to you. You should have no more than 20.

Round 2: Review your 20 words, and cut the list down to 10 values. You can use the blank page to rewrite the 10 to see them all next to each other.

Round 3: From those 10, reduce the list to 5! Reference the tips on the previous page to help you do this.

Once you have uncovered your 5 values, take time to journal the significance of each one in the next section.

Abundance	*A very large quantity of something.*
Acceptance	*Embracing self, others, and circumstance without resistance or judgment.*
Accomplishment	*The successful achievement of a task.*
Adaptability	*The quality of being able to adjust to new conditions.*
Advancement	*Progress toward growth, excellence, and innovation.*
Affection	*Expressing warmth and care through genuine connection.*
Altruism	*Selfless service for the well-being of others.*
Ambition	*Desire and determination to achieve success.*
Assertiveness	*Clearly and respectfully communicating wants, needs, positions, and boundaries.*
Assurance	*Confidence or certainty in one's own abilities.*
Audacity	*Boldly pursuing dreams and taking risks with courage and confidence.*
Awareness	*Knowledge or perception of a situation or fact.*
Balance	*Harmonizing life's priorities with inner peace.*
Beauty	*Recognizing and honoring the goodness in everything.*
Brilliance	*Exceptional talent or intelligence.*
Certainty	*Firm conviction in truth, decisions, and inner knowing.*
Challenge	*Something that puts you to the test.*

Change	*To make or become different.*
Clarity	*The quality of transparency or purity.*
Commitment	*The state or quality of being dedicated to a cause, activity, etc.*
Community	*Connection, support, and shared purpose with others.*
Compassion	*Empathy and kindness towards others' suffering and needs.*
Conformity	*Compliance with standards, rules, or laws.*
Congruency	*Aligning thoughts, actions, and values in harmony.*
Connection	*Building authentic relationships through empathy and understanding.*
Consciousness	*An individual's state of awareness of their environment, thoughts, feelings, or sensations.*
Consistency	*Steady effort and reliability in thoughts and actions over time.*
Conviction	*A firmly held belief or opinion.*
Courage	*Having determination and inner strength in the face of fear.*
Creativity	*Innovative expression through imagination and original ideas.*
Contribution	*Giving time, energy, or resources for others.*
Credibility	*The quality of being trusted and believed in.*
Curiosity	*A strong desire to know or learn something.*
Decisiveness	*Effectively making clear, confident decisions with focused purpose.*

Discipline	*Consistent effort and self-control toward meaningful goals.*
Empathy	*The ability to understand and share the feelings of another.*
Enthusiasm	*Passionate energy driving action and positive influence.*
Fairness	*Impartial and just treatment or behavior without favoritism or discrimination.*
Family	*People who share unconditional love and have long-term commitments to one another.*
Fearlessness	*Courageously facing challenges without hesitation or doubt.*
Fidelity	*Faithfulness to a person, cause, or belief, demonstrated by continuing loyalty.*
Flexibility	*Willingness to change or compromise.*
Friendship	*Genuine connection, support, and trust in others.*
Faith	*Trust and belief in something greater than self.*
Fame	*Recognition through impact, influence, and meaningful contributions.*
Freedom	*the power or right to act, speak, or think as one wants without hindrance or restraint. Autonomy to choose, express, and live authentically.*
Frugality	*Mindful spending, valuing resources, and simplicity.*
Fun	*Enjoyment, amusement, or lighthearted pleasure.*
Generosity	*The quality of being kind and generous.*
Gratitude	*Appreciating life's gifts with a thankful heart.*
Growth	*The ability to develop and mature.*

Health	*The state of being free from illness or injury.*
Honesty	*Fairness and straightforwardness of conduct.*
Imagination	*Forming new ideas and being creative or resourceful.*
Independence	*Not having to depend on anyone or anything else.*
Individuality	*The quality that distinguishes you from others.*
Influence	*The capacity to have an effect on others behavior.*
Integrity	*Having strong moral principles.*
Intellect	*Reasoning and understanding objectively.*
Intimacy	*Deep connection through vulnerability and mutual understanding.*
Introspection	*Examination or observation of one's own mental and emotional processes.*
Intuition	*Instinctive feeling rather than conscious reasoning.*
Justice	*Upholding fairness, equity, and moral integrity.*
Joy	*Embracing positivity, delight, and life's simple pleasures.*
Kindness	*Compassionate actions that uplift and support others.*
Knowledge	*Pursuing understanding and truth through continuous learning.*
Legacy	*Creating lasting impact and meaning for future generations.*
Loyalty	*Devotion, support, and faithfulness to relationships and causes.*

Maturity	Emotional wisdom, responsibility, and thoughtful decision-making.
Meaning	Seeking purpose and significance in life's experiences.
Mindfulness	The quality or state of being conscious or aware of something.
Non-Conformity	Challenging societal expectations boldly by refusing to adhere to a prevailing rule or practice.
Obedience	Respectfully following rules, guidance, and moral principles. Submission to another's authority.
Open-mindedness	Embracing diverse perspectives with curiosity and understanding.
Optimism	Focusing on positivity and hope for future.
Passion	A strong energy, enthusiasm, and dedication for a belief or interest.
Peace	Freedom from disturbance; tranquility, inner calm, harmony, and non-violence.
Performance	Excellence in action, effort, and measurable results.
Power	The ability to direct or influence the behavior of others or the course of events
Play	Engaging in something for enjoyment and recreation with light-heartedness.
Practicality	Prioritizing efficiency, usefulness, and real-world solutions.
Quality	Commitment to excellence, integrity, and superior standards.
Rationality	The quality of being based on or in accordance with reason or logic.
Realism	The attitude or practice of accepting a situation.
Reflection	Contemplating experiences to foster growth and understanding.

Reliability	Consistently dependable in actions, words, and commitments.
Reputation	A widespread belief that someone or something has a particular habit or characteristic.
Resilience	Bouncing back stronger from adversity and challenges.
Resourcefulness	The ability to find quick and clever solutions with available tools and skills.
Respect	Due regard for the feelings, dignity, wishes, rights, perspectives or traditions of others.
Responsibility	Being held accountable for something.
Recognition	Acknowledging efforts and achievements with appreciation.
Self-control	Mastering impulses to align with long-term goals, or to navigate challenges.
Safety	Prioritizing protection for emotional and physical well-being and secure environments.
Selflessness	Concern more with the needs and wishes of others than with one's own.
Self-Reliance	Depending on one's own powers and resources rather than those of others.
Self-Respect	Behaving with honor and dignity.
Sensitivity	Being influenced by a particular thing emotionally or physically.
Sensuality	Appreciating and celebrating something that is pleasing or fulfilling to the senses.
Strength	Resilience and courage in overcoming life's physical, mental, or emotional challenges.
Security	The state of being free from danger or threat.
Spirituality	Connecting to higher purpose through faith and practices.

33

Service	Helping others selflessly with compassion and dedication for the greater good.
Stability	Maintaining balance and consistency.
Trust	To have confidence, faith or hope in someone or something.
Truth	Honoring honesty, authenticity, and alignment with reality.
Teamwork	Collaborating effectively toward common goals and success.
Unity	The state of being joined as a whole.

YOUR TOP 10
VALUES

VALUE REFLECTION

Use the spaces below to list and define your top 5 values. Be generous and specific in your definition. Additionally, allow your definition to include how the value directly impacts how you live in your life. Consider why this value is important to you, and what kind of actions or behaviors are a result of this value or as a result of not upholding this value.

Remember, this isn't about listing the dictionary definition, this is about deeply understanding what this value means to YOU.

VALUE 1:

VALUE 2:

V A L U E   3 :

V A L U E   4 :

V A L U E   5 :

ENERGY AUDIT

It's undeniable that the energy, thoughts, environment, and opinions we surround ourselves with shape how we see the world—and what we believe is possible for ourselves. In this next exercise, you'll have the opportunity to reflect on the things that drain or replenish your energy in each area of your life.

As you reflect, you might find that your community uplifts you, acting as a bridge to your vision for life. Maybe they energize you, love you, and provide the support you need to chase your dreams and goals. Alternatively, you might notice people in your circle who drain your energy, leaving you feeling doubtful or small. Maybe you find yourself spending too much time in public spaces when you would feel much more energized with time alone.

It's important to remember that this exercise isn't about labeling anyone or anything as bad—they're in your life for a reason. This reflection is about YOU. **It's about taking personal responsibility for your time, focus, energy, environment, and relationships and figuring out how you can nurture them and yourself a little more.**

Through this exercise, you'll start to see where you might need to establish firmer boundaries or, on the flip side, where you could incorporate more time doing the activities that really energize and uplift you.

As you complete this reflection, jot down any action steps that come to mind—whether it's sending a thank-you note or making some sort of change to your environment. Hold on to those thoughts; we'll revisit them when we dive into your goals.

RELATIONSHIPS

List the top five to seven people you spend the most time with. What do you notice about your energy after you spend time with them?

What is one word to describe these people? Do any match with your values? Which relationships have helped you grow the most?

What do you love to bring to your relationships?

40

CAREER

What aspects of your work energize you and make you feel excited?

If you had a magic wand, what could you add, change, or remove to feel more aligned?

How aligned do you feel with the values and mission of your current job or career path? Is it that important to you?

41

SPIRITUALITY

What are five words that best describe your current relationship to spirituality?

What practices, routines, or people do you currently engage in to connect with your spirituality?

Have you outgrown any of them? Is there anything new you are excited to try?

ENVIRONMENT

How do you feel about the physical space and town you live in, and does it feel nourishing or draining?

What small changes could you make to your space to feel more energized or inspired?

Are there any sensory elements (like lighting, noise, or smells) that impact your energy at home? Is there anything you'd like to change?

43

SELF

What activities or practices help you reconnect with your authentic self and help you feel expansive or inspired?

What do you wish more people knew about you? How might you let this part of you be known?

How have you learned to trust yourself this year?

44

PHYSICAL BODY

What part of the day do you feel the most tense? Where do you feel that in your body? What part of the day do you feel the most relaxed?

What foods, exercises, or self-care routines make you feel your best? What might you need to shift to make more space for these things?

How do you incorporate rest, recovery, or rejuvenation for your body into your life? If you don't, how might you do this?

45

MENTAL HEALTH

What beliefs, labels, or roles have you outgrown this year, and which ones still feel aligned with who you are today?

Do you notice any recurring patterns of stress or anxiety in your life? What triggers them?

What would it look like to create more space for joy, creativity, and mental peace in your life?

46

MONEY

What are the top five categories that you spend the most money in?
Are they in alignment with your values?

List all of the ways money comes into your life. Do you like receiving
money in this way? Would you like to add or remove income streams?

How often do you spend money on things that bring you genuine joy
and satisfaction?

47

SECTION 3
THE NEW YEAR

JOURNAL PROMPTS FOR THE NEW YEAR

How do you want to feel in your day-to-day life? Are there any parts of yourself that want to come out of hiding this year?

JOURNAL PROMPTS FOR THE NEW YEAR

If you focused on only one thing for this upcoming year, what do you think would be the most impactful? Why?

JOURNAL PROMPTS FOR THE NEW YEAR

Do you have any resistance to prioritizing that thing? If so, where is the resistance coming from?

BRAIN DUMP

Use this space for unfiltered reflection or as an outline for what you desire for the new year. Draw, doodle, dance, write a poem— however you'd like to express the possibilities for your future.

54

CELEBRATING YOU

Moving toward your intentions means stepping into the unknown. There is an edge you must face; the choice to begin thinking, speaking, and living in a new way or continue what you have been doing.

This edge might sound scary, but it's also miraculous. At the edge anything is possible. You cannot see beyond the edge because you haven't been there. It might be the edge of a cliff or the edge of a beautiful forest. Whatever it is, the edge is the place where we can choose to step forward into a new version of ourselves, and maybe grow wings.

The human part of us will likely see the edge and sound the alarm, urging us to turn around and run back to what is familiar. This alarm can show up in various ways—most commonly through anxious thoughts and behaviors, lovingly referred to as "Protection Patterns." These patterns are fueled by fear—the part of us that prioritizes safety and survival.

Protection Patterns aren't something to be ashamed of; they're simply mechanisms designed to do what their name suggests—protect us. Protection Patterns often stem from a younger version of yourself that was taught, either by people or experience, to be afraid. While shifting these patterns is a simple process, it does require loving practice and patience.

This section has two parts to help you remember your truth in the face of fear. The first is creating a sketch or drawing of your authentic self. The second is a five-step journaling process that you can come back to when you begin to face resistance or fear in your new year.

Remember, the only time you can choose to be courageous is when you are afraid.

Inquire within, rather than without, asking:

'What part of myself do I wish to experience now?'

'What aspects of being do I choose to call forth?'

For all of life exists as a tool of your own creation, and all of its events merely present themselves as opportunities for you to decide, and be, Who You Are."

— Neale Donald Walsch

CELEBRATING YOU

Use this space to describe or illustrate your most authentic self - what are your most true and loving thoughts about yourself and the world? What are the most loving actions you take or words you speak? How does it feel for others to be around you?

5 STEPS TO WORK THROUGH PROTECTION PATTERNS:

STEP 1: IDENTIFY

Identify the thought or action that is incongruent with your authentic self:

STEP 2: UNCOVER THE FEAR

What is the fear underneath the thought or action?

STEP 3: UNDERSTANDING

What if this fear is an old friend. How is it protecting you?
(*Example: "I'm not good enough" = "I don't want to be rejected."*)

STEP 4: DIALOGUE

Give your fear the pen, and invite it to share what it is afraid of and what it needs from you to be safe. *(Tip: Try writing with your non-dominant hand)*

STEP 5: COMPASSION

Give the pen back to your authentic self and invite this version of you to respond to the fear with compassion. What truth do you want it to know? How can you let your fear know that it's been heard?

INTENTION SETTING
The "Why" Behind the "What"

The process of creating an intention is one of the best exercises to reconnect with your authenticity. This is because a powerful intention prioritizes your personal growth and encourages you to look a layer deeper than basic goal setting does.

However, for many, it can be challenging to feel safe in their full self-expression due to our unique trauma history, social influence, and family conditioning.

The way most of us have been taught to set and achieve goals comes at a cost. We have been taught that we must sacrifice something: our life force energy, our time, our boundaries, or something else, in order to create success. It seems all too often, we are only celebrated in our society if we've become a martyr for our goals, and this internalized lie has us judging the quality of our success by how much was sacrificed to get there, or even blurring the definition of success altogether.

Success becomes elusive, and we become drained, disconnected, and constantly in search of external validation.

61   *© Copyright Annabelle Dura*

Essentially, the world out there is wild, and setting an intention through this embodied process brings you back home to your authenticity. Most importantly this gives you the compass you need to navigate through the noise of the old paradigm and begin connecting and fulfilling your life's calling for the year ahead and beyond. Ultimately, it allows you to dance in a beautiful, fulfilling, inspiring co-creation with the universe.

The prolific Joseph Campbell wrote **"If you can see your path laid out in front of you, then you know it's not your path. Your own path is made with every step you take..."**

Your purpose calls you into uncharted territory. But we can't successfully navigate new territory without a guide or a compass. Your intention is that compass; the thing you can count on to steer you in the right direction when faced with challenging decisions or exciting new opportunities.

Throughout this workbook, you've met the challenges meant to help you cultivate a relationship with your inner compass. Now it's time to begin the first step in your intention-setting process. Remember, the more specific you can be with each step, the better. The more specific your intention is, the more powerful it will feel when you read it, and the clearer it is for the universe to work with!

Belonging so fully to yourself that you're willing to stand alone is a wilderness—an untamed, unpredictable place of solitude and searching. It is a place as dangerous as it is breathtaking, a place as sought after as it is feared.

The wilderness can often feel unholy because we can't control it, or what people think about our choice of whether to venture into that vastness or not. But it turns out to be the place of true belonging, and it's the bravest and most sacred place you will ever stand.

- Brené Brown

1 START WITH YOU

What is the **one character trait** or **value** that would lay the foundation for all of the beautiful things that you desire in the upcoming year?

This step is **internal** or **identity-based**. Your one thing is all about who you must become to live the life you desire. You may want to select a value from your list or choose an entirely separate word or phrase.

On the next page, set a seven-minute timer and journal about the person you desire to be at the end of this upcoming year.

As you journal, you might consider the following questions: When you embody this character trait or value, what kind of things do you do? What do you believe in? What do you value? Feel free to write or draw!

IDENTITY REFLECTION
WHO WILL I BECOME?

2 SACRED COMMITMENTS

Your sacred commitments are the external action you will take to support your one thing. Achieve X (your one thing) through Y (your sacred commitments). **What are 1-2 tangible actions you can take on a daily basis to support this?**

The key here is to keep your commitments simple and small so they feel super easy to show up for.

This is less about accomplishment and more about creating the habits that support your intention. You are acting in alignment with the person you desire to become.

Use the space on the following page to articulate how these sacred commitment will impact your intention.

67

MY SACRED COMMITMENTS

68

3 IMPACT

As your intention begins to actualize through your sacred commitments, **what else in your life will it impact?** Powerful intentions don't have limits. Your intention will touch all parts of your life as it comes to be, because **you** are the common denominator. Your intention is the stone in the pond and these are the ripples. As your intention comes closer to you, you will start to notice some of the shifts in other parts of your life, as if the universe is dropping little clues around you to encourage you to keep going.

EXAMPLE

An intention to increase self-love might mean you setting boundaries at work, allowing you to be more focused and at peace, which leads to higher quality work and eventually a raise. In this example, the intention touches relationships, career, and finances!

IMPACT REFLECTION
THE RIPPLE EFFECT

4 FEELING STATES

Next, write your feeling states. I recommend listing anywhere between three to five **powerful feelings or emotions** you'll experience as your intention manifests. Your feeling might be peace or joy. It might also sound like: *I feel softness in my face and chest.* The feeling states are one of the most important pieces because they are a reminder that these feelings are accessible to you now. Whenever you feel disconnected from your intention, you can access your feeling states by meditating on them or doing the action step below to bring you closer to it.

ACTION ITEM

One by one, embody the feeling states you listed as fully as possible. Set a one-minute timer to let yourself feel one feeling. When the timer goes off, reset it & feel through the next feeling.

MY FEELING STATES

72

5 IT'S NOT JUST ABOUT YOU

Finally, when your intention comes to life, how is it a blessing for those around you? I love this part because it is such a powerful reminder that **you living as your most authentic self is good—not just for you, but for everyone around you too!** Consider your friends, your family, and the people in your workplace or community. List all of the ways that your intention is impactful, supportive, or inspiring to them. After this step, use the next page to put it all together!

ACTION ITEM

Share your intention with someone you trust, close your eyes and send love to your intention together! Don't want to share with someone? Read it to yourself out loud in the mirror.

MY HIGHEST GOOD IS
GOOD FOR OTHERS

74

6 PUT IT ALL TOGETHER

You now have all of the parts of your intention! Use the outline written below to lovingly combine all of these pieces into one powerful intention on the next page.

Part 1: It is my intention that in this coming year I... (*What is your "one trait" intention for this year?*)

Part 2: I am able to bring this intention to life by... (*Insert sacred commitments.*)

Part 3: When I experience my intention come to life, I feel... (*Write feelings in the present tense.*)

Part 4: My intention coming true and me feeling this way is good for the whole world because...

Part 5: Select an image, word, or phrase to represent your intention. Draw or write it.

MY NEW YEAR *INTENTION*

76

GOAL SETTING
FUEL THE FIRE

It's time to move into action! In this section, you have a goal sheet for every area of life, and a few extra blank ones. Each sheet has a section to circle which quarter you will focus on for this goal. You will **not** tackle all of these goals at once. Instead, you will choose which goals to focus on and when.

Decide if you prefer to focus on only one goal at a time, or multiple, but **do not choose more than three per quarter.** This will help you feel confident, capable, and clear as you move forward into your new year.

Goal Setting Tips:
- **Simplify simplify simplify!** If you start to feel confused or overwhelmed, ask yourself: *How do I make this simpler and more specific?*
- **Start small.** Small steps are still steps! The more attainable your goal, the more likely you'll achieve and succeed. Remember, it all counts toward your bigger vision, and you can increase the challenge later.
- **Hold your goals with open hands.** Not completing a goal doesn't mean you're a failure. Consistency is important but our society tends to over-emphasize it. The goals you set align you with your truth. If you eventually find that they are no longer moving you toward what you desire, let them go.

GOALS

Outline the main goal for this area of your life for the new year. This can be something you want to achieve, something you want to experience, or something you just want to grow in.

RELATIONSHIPS

Goal:

This is important to me because...

When will you focus on this?
(Circle one)

Q1   Q2   Q3   Q4

Break It Down: What can I do to accomplish this goal by my deadline? What will I need to focus on daily?

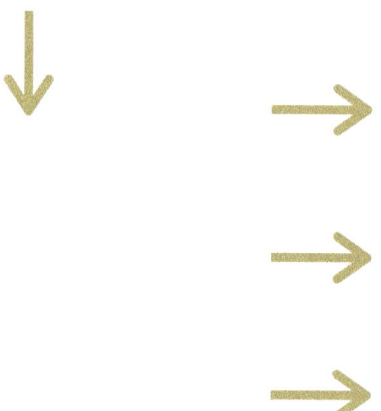

ACTION PLAN:

   Schedule It

   Set Reminders

   Find an Accountability Buddy.

GOALS

Outline the main goal for this area of your life for the new year. This can be something you want to achieve, something you want to experience, or something you just want to grow in.

CAREER

Goal:

This is important to me because...

When will you focus on this?
(Circle one)

Q1   Q2   Q3   Q4

Break It Down: What can I do to accomplish this goal by my deadline? What will I need to focus on daily?

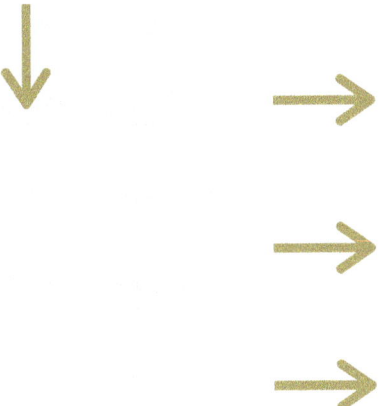

ACTION PLAN:

- Schedule It
- Set Reminders
- Find an Accountability Buddy.

GOALS

Outline the main goal for this area of your life for the new year. This can be something you want to achieve, something you want to experience, or something you just want to grow in.

SELF

Goal:

This is important to me because...

When will you focus on this?
(Circle one)

Q1   Q2   Q3   Q4

Break It Down: What can I do to accomplish this goal by my deadline? What will I need to focus on daily?

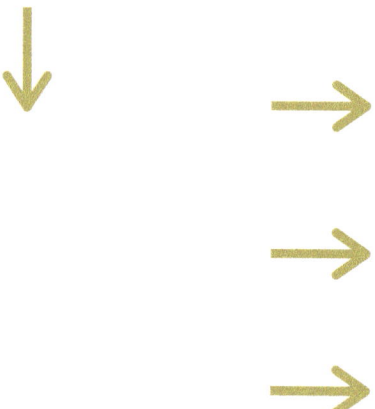

ACTION PLAN:

- Schedule It
- Set Reminders
- Find an Accountability Buddy.

GOALS

Outline the main goal for this area of your life for the new year. This can be something you want to achieve, something you want to experience, or something you just want to grow in.

PHYSICAL HEALTH

Goal:

This is important to me because...

When will you focus on this?
(Circle one)

Q1   Q2   Q3   Q4

Break It Down: What can I do to accomplish this goal by my deadline? What will I need to focus on daily?

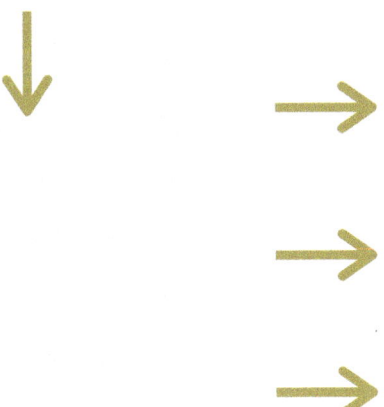

ACTION PLAN:

- Schedule It
- Set Reminders
- Find an Accountability Buddy.

GOALS

Outline the main goal for this area of your life for the new year. This can be something you want to achieve, something you want to experience, or something you just want to grow in.

MENTAL HEALTH

Goal:

This is important to me because...

When will you focus on this?
(Circle one)

Q1   Q2   Q3   Q4

Break It Down: What can I do to accomplish this goal by my deadline? What will I need to focus on daily?

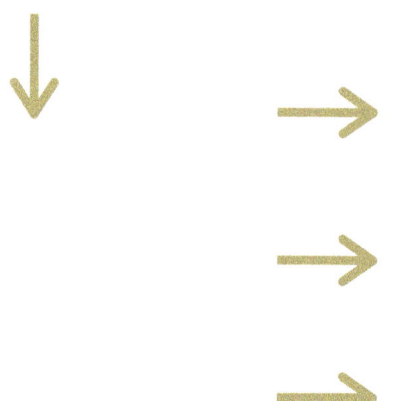

ACTION PLAN:

Schedule It

Set Reminders

Find an Accountability Buddy.

GOALS

Outline the main goal for this area of your life for the new year. This can be something you want to achieve, something you want to experience, or something you just want to grow in.

ENVIRONMENT

Goal:

This is important to me because...

When will you focus on this?
(Circle one)

Q1   Q2   Q3   Q4

Break It Down: What can I do to accomplish this goal by my deadline? What will I need to focus on daily?

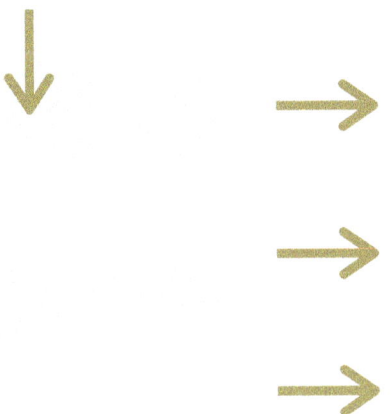

ACTION PLAN:

☐ Schedule It

☐ Set Reminders

☐ Find an Accountability Buddy.

GOALS

Outline the main goal for this area of your life for the new year. This can be something you want to achieve, something you want to experience, or something you just want to grow in.

MONEY

Goal:

This is important to me because...

When will you focus on this?
(Circle one)

Q1   Q2   Q3   Q4

Break It Down: What can I do to accomplish this goal by my deadline? What will I need to focus on daily?

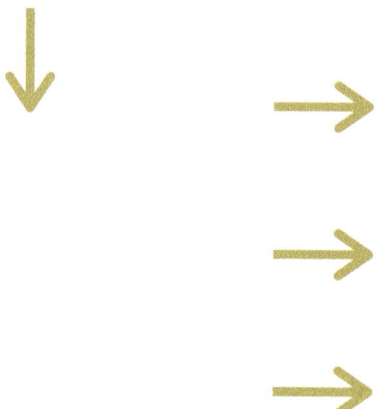

ACTION PLAN:

- Schedule It
- Set Reminders
- Find an Accountability Buddy.

GOALS

Outline the main goal for this area of your life for the new year. This can be something you want to achieve, something you want to experience, or something you just want to grow in.

SPIRITUALITY

Goal:

This is important to me because...

When will you focus on this?
(Circle one)

Q1   Q2   Q3   Q4

Break It Down: What can I do to accomplish this goal by my deadline? What will I need to focus on daily?

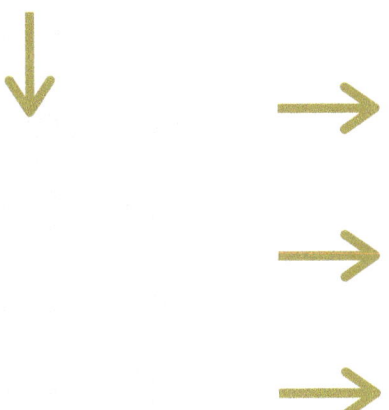

ACTION PLAN:

- Schedule It
- Set Reminders
- Find an Accountability Buddy.

GOALS

Outline the main goal for this area of your life for the new year. This can be something you want to achieve, something you want to experience, or something you just want to grow in.

Goal:

This is important to me because...

When will you focus on this?
(Circle one)

Q1   Q2   Q3   Q4

Break It Down: What can I do to accomplish this goal by my deadline? What will I need to focus on daily?

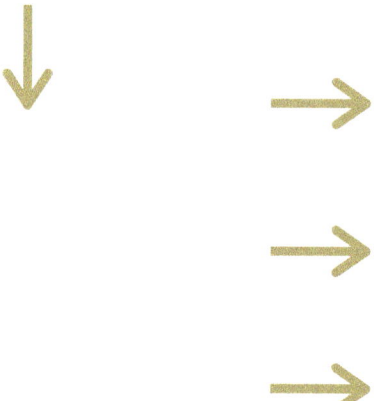

ACTION PLAN:

- Schedule It
- Set Reminders
- Find an Accountability Buddy.

GOALS

Outline the main goal for this area of your life for the new year. This can be something you want to achieve, something you want to experience, or something you just want to grow in.

Goal:

This is important to me because...

When will you focus on this?
(Circle one)   **Q1   Q2   Q3   Q4**

Break It Down: What can I do to accomplish this goal by my deadline? What will I need to focus on daily?

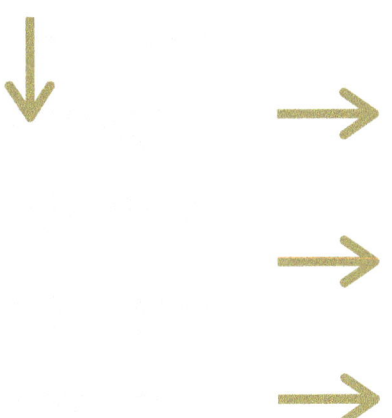

ACTION PLAN:

Schedule It

Set Reminders

Find an Accountability Buddy.

GOALS

Outline the main goal for this area of your life for the new year. This can be something you want to achieve, something you want to experience, or something you just want to grow in.

Goal:

This is important to me because...

When will you focus on this?
(Circle one)

Q1 Q2 Q3 Q4

Break It Down: What can I do to accomplish this goal by my deadline? What will I need to focus on daily?

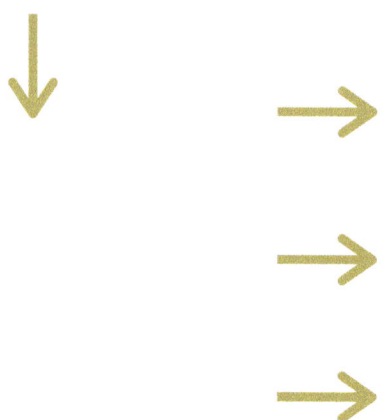

ACTION PLAN:

Schedule It

Set Reminders

Find an Accountability Buddy.

GOALS

Outline the main goal for this area of your life for the new year. This can be something you want to achieve, something you want to experience, or something you just want to grow in.

Goal:

This is important to me because...

When will you focus on this?
(Circle one)
                                    # Q1   Q2   Q3   Q4

Break It Down: What can I do to accomplish this goal by my deadline? What will I need to focus on daily?

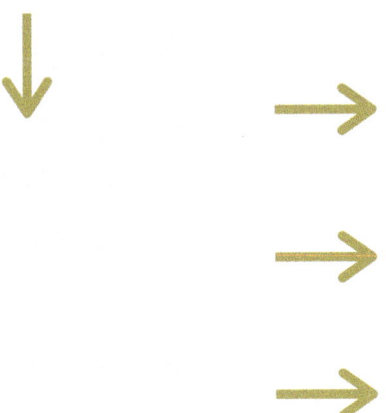

ACTION PLAN:

 Schedule It

 Set Reminders

 Find an Accountability Buddy.

GOALS

Outline the main goal for this area of your life for the new year. This can be something you want to achieve, something you want to experience, or something you just want to grow in.

Goal:

This is important to me because...

When will you focus on this?
(Circle one)

Q1   Q2   Q3   Q4

Break It Down: What can I do to accomplish this goal by my deadline? What will I need to focus on daily?

ACTION PLAN:

Schedule It

Set Reminders

Find an Accountability Buddy.

GOALS

Outline the main goal for this area of your life for the new year. This can be something you want to achieve, something you want to experience, or something you just want to grow in.

Goal:

This is important to me because...

When will you focus on this?
(Circle one)

Q1   Q2   Q3   Q4

Break It Down: What can I do to accomplish this goal by my deadline? What will I need to focus on daily?

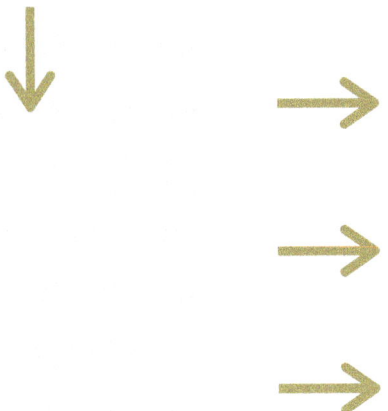

ACTION PLAN:

- Schedule It
- Set Reminders
- Find an Accountability Buddy.

A LETTER FROM THE AUTHOR

Dear Beautiful Human,

Thank you, from the depths of my heart, for opening up these pages, and allowing some of the love I put into this workbook to touch your life.

Even if you didn't complete all of the prompts or even if it took you multiple months to read the first page, I hope it inspired you to take a little bit of time for YOU.

In seasons of deep questioning in my own life, times when I was feeling lost, disconnected, and uninspired, it was the consistent practice of journaling that brought me back home inside of myself.

It's often the many quiet, thoughtful, and sometimes tearful hours spent alone with a journal that change the course of a day, a week, a year, or a whole life. I know it has changed mine.

I'm so full of joy thinking about the work you've done here, and how it will serve your beautiful vision. I'm so grateful this journal got to be a footnote in your story.

My deepest wish for you from this moment on is that you continue to cultivate and trust your own inner power. Remember that everything you desire to create for your beautiful, authentic life this year is possible.

Now stop reading, turn on your favorite song, and DANCE! You deserve a celebration!

Annabelle ♥

www.ingramcontent.com/pod-product-compliance
Lightning Source LLC
Chambersburg PA
CBHW041539120626
46551CB00019B/2761